GW00730675

THE MANUAL²

FIGHTERS/KEEPERS/ LOSERS/REAPERS

CARL BEECH WITH
ROY CROWNE
AND ALEX WILLMOTT

Carl

Carl is married to Karen and has two daughters. He's the leader of CVM (an international men's movement) and the founder of 'the code'. Previously a banker, church planter and senior pastor, he is convinced he is a great chef, plays the piano, loves cycling, movies and sci-fi books and caught a record-breaking catfish on the river Ebro in Spain.

Twitter @carlfbeech

Roy

Having worked for Youth for Christ for 28 years, Roy then became co-founder of Hope 08, alongside Andy Hawthorne and Mike Pilavachi, and is now the Executive Director of Hope, a mission initiative in words and action, with the Church working together for the next three years to 2014. He loves to preach, teach and see the Church being good news in order to bring about transformation. Roy lives in Rugby with his wife, and they have two sons.

Alex

Alex is a 27-year-old former newspaper reporter who heads up the communications department for Christian Vision for Men. He is from Merthyr Tydfil, South Wales, and enjoys football, rugby union, golf and snooker. Alex became a follower of Jesus when he was 16 years old and has recently written a fantasy novel called *Selah* which is available on the Amazon Kindle.

Contents

BOOK 2

[INTRO]

We've finally cracked it!
After being asked to write daily notes for men a number of times over the years, we've finally nailed it. So, in a nutshell, here you go and let the journey begin!

It's a simple and well-proven approach. The notes are between 150–300 words long. Each day begins with a verse and ends in a prayer. It will take you no more than a few minutes to read but I hope that what you read stays in your head throughout your day. The notes are numbered rather than dated, so it's OK if you miss a day to pick it back up. If you want to study with a group of guys you can easily keep track of where you are up to or swap ideas on that particular study online (we've a Facebook page). If you want to be part of a band of brothers internationally swapping thoughts, insights and prayer requests then you can do that as well by using our new Facebook page.

In each issue, I've asked some of my mates to contribute. In this one, big thanks go to Roy Crowne and Alex Willmott for their insights and thoughts. They're both great guys going after God's heart. We really hope that the subjects from Fighters to Reapers really speak in all of our lives and help us stay on the narrow path!

So there it is. The Word of God has such power to inform and transform our lives, so let's knuckle down and get reading.

Your brother in Christ
Carl

[FIGHTERS]

01/Bloody-minded

'Next to him was Eleazar son of Dodai the Ahohite. As one of the three mighty warriors, he was with David when they taunted the Philistines gathered at Pas Dammim for battle. Then the Israelites retreated, but Eleazar stood his ground and struck down the Philistines till his hand grew tired and froze to the sword.'
2 Samuel 23:9-10

David's mighty men were the biblical equivalent of Special Forces. These guys were off the chart when it came to warfare, heroism and all-round testosterone-fuelled escapades. First up we have Eleazar (I'm missing out Josheb-Basshebeth because it's hard to base a devotional solely on the fact that he killed 800 men in one battle with a spear! I suggest you read the whole chapter).

The line that jumps out at me when I read about Eleazar is that his hand 'froze to the sword'.

Basically, he didn't quit. He hung in there until the job was done, clearly to the point of exhaustion. Now, obviously we aren't facing hordes of marauding Philistines, but we do have our own battles and challenges. I've often noticed that men have a real tendency to give up too quickly when the going gets tough. Perhaps there was a vision God gave you to do something but you feel like quitting because it's hard? Perhaps there's a situation at work or a relationship you feel like giving up on? Let me put this to you today: Have you stood your ground until your hand has frozen to the sword? Sometimes we just need to grit our teeth and be a bit bloody-minded. I wonder how much good stuff doesn't happen because us guys quit too quickly.

Prayer: Father, develop within me a bloody-minded spirit that doesn't quit at the first sign of trouble but is tenacious and gritty, so that I may better serve You. Amen.

02/Lentils

'Next to him was Shammah son of Agee the Hararite. When the Philistines banded together at a place where there was a field full of lentils, Israel's troops fled from them. But Shammah took his stand in the middle of the field. He defended it and struck the Philistines down, and the LORD brought about a great victory.'
2 Samuel 23:11-12

Some commentaries written by people with theological brains the size of small planetary systems have various theories about why Shammah decided to make a stand in a field full of lentils. None of them suggest that it's anything to do with militant vegetarianism, but they do conjecture that perhaps it was because lentils were a valuable crop. Now, I'm a simple man and I've got my own simple theory and I don't think we need to dwell on the lentils too much. The point is this: the enemy was advancing and

Shammah was having none of it. He drew a line on the ground and decided that no Philistine was going to cross it. Often as men we need to draw such a line and hold it. We just need to decide which field it's going to be in and what our lentils are! Perhaps it's the banter in the office, or the slightly inflated expenses claims that people around you put in. Maybe it's stuff you're looking at that you know deep down you shouldn't be. Whatever you resolve to make your field of lentils, fight hard and don't let the enemy cross the line!

Prayer: Show me where I must no longer compromise. Give me the courage to draw the line and the strength to make my stand. Amen.

03/Water

'During harvest time, three of the thirty chief warriors came down to David at the cave of Adullam, while a band of Philistines was encamped in the Valley of Rephaim. At that time David was in the stronghold, and the Philistine garrison was at Bethlehem. David longed for water and said, "Oh, that someone would get me a drink of water from the well near the gate of Bethlehem!" So the three mighty warriors broke through the Philistine lines, drew water from the well near the gate of Bethlehem and carried it back to David. But he refused to drink it; instead, he poured it out before the LORD. "Far be it from me, LORD, to do this!" he said. "Is it not the blood of men who went at the risk of their lives?" And David would not drink it.' **2 Samuel 23:13-17**

At first reading, I wondered if the mighty men would have been a bit hacked off. There they were, risking their lives to break through enemy lines so they could get the guv'nor a drink and all he does is pour it away. It almost looks ungrateful!

It's not, though. What we are seeing here is a huge overflow of emotion. These guys lived, ate, slept, fought and survived together. They faced huge threats together as a band of brothers. And so, at this moment, David is overcome by the honour they have given him and he wants to give it back. Honouring others is, at its best, a mutual thing. It isn't taught very much these days, but it's so critical to a kingdom lifestyle. It means not pulling down our leaders (something we do far too often). It means showing respect to all people at all times. In fact, we should be outdoing one another in giving honour. Wouldn't the world look different if we all lived that way?

Prayer: Forgive me for the times when I've been less than honourable. Help me to learn from the example of David's mighty men and live it out among the people I know. Help me to give honour to those who lead me. Amen.

[WISE UP!]

04/ Weights and measures

'The LORD detests dishonest scales, but accurate weights find favour with him.' **Proverbs 11:1**

The principle here is that God loves honesty. It's just so easy to cross the line sometimes. Just have a ponder on these mini-scenarios. I can save a bit by paying cash and avoiding VAT. I can inflate my expenses a little and make a few quid. I can slightly understate my tax liability on my self-assessment form. I can put a few hours extra on my time sheet. I can claim overtime when I didn't really do any. And so it goes on – and, bit by bit, the more we blur the line between honesty and dishonesty, the more we blunt the work of the Holy Spirit in our lives and the more we grieve God.

Of course, sometimes it's not just getting a bit of extra cash that can derail us. I remember once being asked to cheat in front of some work colleagues in my bank and having to really fight to cross the pain barrier to say no, as I didn't want to look like the squeaky-clean, cheesy Christian guy. Sometimes though, you just have to hold the line. It's tough to be the honest one and harder still to play it straight all the time; but that's the call of the kingdom and that's what it means to walk on the narrow road.

Prayer: Keep my heart honest and my path straight. Amen.

05/Don't be a plonker!

'When pride comes, then comes disgrace, but with humility comes wisdom.' **Proverbs 11:2**

There's some good stuff here for blokes. We do suffer really badly from pride. We hate to be wrong and we love to be respected and admired. Solomon nails it here, though. Go through life full of pride and the inevitable fall will happen. And as you won't have made many friends along the way (because pride isn't the most attractive of qualities), when you do come tumbling down the impact will probably be hard. Most pride is driven by insecurity – and that makes a toxic combination. If you are an insecure, proud person, pray that God takes hold of this weakness, or else it will take hold of you.

The flip side in this verse is humility. The humble are wise, it says – probably because the humble are slow to speak and quick to listen. They don't think too highly of themselves and therefore are willing to learn and are not afraid to surround themselves with people who are better or more able than they are. (Proud men never surround themselves with people who are better than them at anything!) So, keep a healthy perspective on yourself – it's the only way forward!

Prayer: Please deal with any pride in my heart and teach me how to live humbly. Amen.

06/ Liar, liar!

'The integrity of the upright guides them, but the unfaithful are destroyed by their duplicity.'
Proverbs 11:3

Tell a lie and you end up telling another lie to cover your tracks. Keep going that way and before long you'll forget what's fact and what's fiction. It's dangerous territory for a whole number of reasons. Police or intelligence agents working undercover have to have really close oversight to make sure that they don't fall foul of their own deception. There's only so much duplicity a person can engage in before they 'blow up'. The thing is, tell a lie and you may get away with it for a while, but keep going like that and it will get you in the end. Even if you don't get found out, something inside you will die. It's hard to live with the fact that you have lied. I've known people come to me after many years, needing to deal with their guilt. We just weren't meant to operate in that way. It's dangerous for your emotional and spiritual health.

The Bible here is completely unambiguous: live with deception and it will destroy you. Just think about the classic scenario of adultery. For a few moments of pleasure, it's very likely that once you're found out, your whole world will come crashing down. (Those not married, just take note!) So, keep it honest, and keep your integrity.

Prayer: Forgive me for any lies I tell, and for any deception in my heart or my actions. May my life be characterised by integrity, not duplicity. Amen.

07/No snipers

'A gossip betrays a confidence, but a trustworthy person keeps a secret.'
Proverbs 11:13

Do blokes gossip? Of course they do, but it's probably better described as sniping and slandering. Gossip takes many forms, but in a nutshell it's simply sharing information about someone else that you shouldn't. It's often based on mere hearsay, and it's usually meant to inflict damage. When someone starts to tell me something about someone that obviously has been picked up on the grapevine or told them for their ears only, my instant reaction is to think that I probably can't really trust that person with anything. After all, if they're happy to talk to me out of turn, what might they say or pass on about me? Gossip is toxic.

The other thing about it is, it's destructive for all concerned. Invariably, it's never going to be helpful to the person you're talking about and it's only going to damage your integrity, in the eyes of God and possibly of others. So: don't do it – and if someone starts sniping about someone else to you, tell 'em to put a sock in it! We are called to be men of integrity whose 'yes' means yes and whose 'no' means no, and that's it. So, ensure that your words bring life and not despair and death.

Prayer: Make me a man whose words bring life and not death. Help me to be known as a guy who speaks only well of people and never destructively. Amen.

08/Wiser heads

'For lack of guidance a nation falls, but victory is won through many advisors.' **Proverbs 11:14**

If you want to look into this a bit deeper, check out the story in 1 Kings 12. In a nutshell, Solomon dies and his son Rehoboam takes over. Immediately, a group representing the people of Israel, led by a guy called Jeroboam, appeals to the new king to lower their taxes. The older, wiser men who worked with Solomon advise Rehoboam to take it easy, listen to their case and be considerate. The younger guys, his peers, however, tell him to go for it and make life even tougher for the people. Rehoboam ignores the men who worked with his dad and winds up provoking a rebellion. End result? The kingdom is split into two, with Israel in the north and Judah in the south – Rehoboam getting much the smaller part!

Taking advice from those who have gone before us is crucial. Surround yourself with wisdom. Spend time with those you don't instinctively agree with. Don't give a hearing only to those who are like you and agree with you all the time – a 'yes man' culture leads to decline. Listen to the stories of the past and learn from everyone you can. Don't, don't, don't fall into the trap of being a Rehoboam! A good and wise leader – a good and wise man – always takes wise counsel.

Prayer: Help me to be slow to speak and eager to learn. Help me to bring into my life men who are older and wiser in the faith and learn to listen to those around me who will help me make good decisions. Amen.

09/Home truths

> 'Whoever loves discipline loves knowledge, but whoever hates correction is stupid.' **Proverbs 12:1**

It's tough when someone takes you aside and points out the error of your ways. It's hard to take correction on the chin and harder still to reflect on it and make the necessary changes. I've been on the receiving end of 'advice' many times and sometimes the way it's delivered to you can be incredibly frustrating and even painful; but you have to look past that. There will be those who tell you the truth for unkind and unhelpful reasons and those who do so because they want the best for you and from you. You can learn from both if you keep your head.

Let's have a ponder on something the great preacher Spurgeon once said:

'Get a friend to tell you your faults, or, better still, welcome an enemy who will watch you keenly and sting you savagely. What a blessing such

an irritating critic will be to a wise man, what an intolerable nuisance to a fool! Correct yourself diligently and frequently, or you will fall into errors unawares, false tones will grow, and slovenly habits will form insensibly; therefore criticize yourself with unceasing care.'

Taking it on the chin is a necessary part of growing more Christlike. I think we can leave it at that ...

Prayer: When I'm criticised, help me to take the best from it and ignore what is toxic. Surround me with those who care enough about me to tell me some hard truths when needed. Amen.

10/Cool it!

'A quick-tempered person does
foolish things, and the one who
devises evil schemes is hated.'
Proverbs 14:17

We've probably all been there. You get into a row
with someone and before you know it, something
has come out of your mouth that you instantly
regret. The same thing with emails. How many
times have you seen this happen? You get an
email that does your head in and without pausing
for thought you smash out a reply and hit 'send' –
only to be struck a few minutes later by a sinking
feeling that maybe that email didn't mean quite
what you thought after all! Or perhaps you get
hit by an overwhelming sense of regret because
you've just taken the whole exchange to an
unnecessary eruption of open warfare. The
problem then is that, unless you step back, you
end up plotting your next move – and, as the Bible
says here, that's not a fast route to being well-
liked! Us blokes need to really master the art of
taking a long, deep breath. React to a dispute or

an injustice immediately and you'll be on a hiding to nothing. Sometimes you just need to sleep on it. You'll find yourself cooling down and certainly getting a different perspective on things.

Prayer: Make me a man of peace and not war. Refine my character so that I am known more for thinking things through than for being reactive and vindictive. Amen.

A quick temper will make a fool of you soon enough.
BRUCE LEE

I don't lose my temper often; about once every twenty years perhaps.
DIRK BOGARDE

11/Drawing the line

'But Daniel resolved not to defile himself with the royal food and wine, and he asked the chief official for permission not to defile himself in this way.' **Daniel 1:8**

So, here we have it: a classic case of drawing a line in the sand. King Nebuchadnezzar has taken Daniel and some others captive. They've been ripped from their homes, their people, their customs and language. Everything is now unfamiliar. It's also pretty likely they've been castrated as well, as only eunuchs served in the Babylonian king's palace! However, Daniel makes a resolution and I believe it is one reason why God blesses him, not only at this point but throughout his life. He decides not to eat food offered to idols. Note that he doesn't do it in a confrontational way – in fact, he actually asks for permission! He just quietly resolves to draw a line in the sand and honour God where and when he can.

It's an inspiring story for us guys. With so many pressures out there to tolerate shades of grey, we would do well to make some concrete decisions about the places we go, the things we say and the stuff we do. One thing's for sure: you are more likely to see God bless you for holding the line than for living with compromise.

Prayer: Show me where I need to draw a line and no longer compromise so that I might glorify You by the way I conduct my life. Help me to be as passionate as Daniel in the pursuit of righteousness. Amen.

12/Facing the heat

'Shadrach, Meshach and Abednego replied to him, "King Nebuchadnezzar, we do not need to defend ourselves before you in this matter. If we are thrown into the blazing furnace, the God we serve is able to deliver us from it, and he will deliver us from Your Majesty's hand. But even if he does not, we want you to know, Your Majesty, that we will not serve your gods or worship the image of gold you have set up."' **Daniel 3:16-18**

Three guys are to be put to death for refusing to worship the image of gold that King Nebuchadnezzar has set up. Absolutely seething with rage, the king makes it a simple choice: they either fall to the floor and worship the image or it's instant death by very large BBQ. For Shadrach, Meshach and Abednego, it's not a complicated decision. Their answer is pretty much 'Stuff you and your gold image!' What really floors me and so many people when they read this story is the total calmness with which they approach their decision. In a sense, what they're saying is this: 'Win, lose or draw, it's cool. God can save us – but if He doesn't want to, that's fine by us as well!'

So, what is it they've got that I don't think many of us have (and certainly not me)? In a nutshell, I think it's a robust understanding that God is good. No matter what happens to them, they know that God loves them and is for them and that, whatever happens, they can trust Him. For us now, post-resurrection with the promise of eternity, we have the additional benefit of being able to say 'it is well with my soul'. I really like that! Imagine what life would be like for us if we really grasped that God is good in the way these guys did!

Prayer: I know, God, that You are good and that Your love endures for ever. I know that You are for us and not against us. Help that understanding to filter through into the activity of my everyday life. Amen.

13/Singed

'Then King Nebuchadnezzar leaped to his feet in amazement and asked his advisors, "Weren't there three men that we tied up and threw into the fire?" They replied, "Certainly, Your Majesty." He said, "Look! I see four men walking around in the fire, unbound and unharmed, and the fourth looks like a son of the gods."' `Daniel 3:24-25`

This is a reminder to us guys that God is sovereign and can do whatever He likes, whenever He chooses to do it. It's so easy to forget the supernatural dimension of what we believe. Us men can be so matter-of-fact and so driven by logic and the need for proof, we can often slam the door on living with the expectation that God is a God of the sometimes crazily unexpected. Shadrach, Meshach and Abednego honoured God and He honoured them. A clearly furnace-proof angel was sent in to unbind them and they were completely untouched – not even a singed eyebrow between them. Fantastic!

There are a huge number of stories of angelic protection out there and we don't have time or space to retell them here. So, for now, let's just remind ourselves that we aren't alone in whatever we are facing, particularly if we are making a stand for God. He is with us and His angels are on constant standby should they need to be scrambled to our rescue. So, let's get out there and face the day and whatever fiery furnace you might have in front of you!

Prayer: Thank You, God, that You are the God of supernatural intervention. Thank You that You are all-powerful and more than able to deal with whatever problems or obstacles are put in my way. Help me to remember this next time I find myself in a spot of bother as a result of my faith! Amen.

14/Taking a stand

'Now when Daniel learned that the decree had been published, he went home to his upstairs room where the windows opened towards Jerusalem. Three times a day he got down on his knees and prayed, giving thanks to his God, just as he had done before.' **Daniel 6:10**

It's 'no compromise' time again for Daniel. He's not a man to go down without a fight when his faith is the target. Another edict has been passed, this time banning him from praying to the God of Israel. He's having none of it, though, and as a result he gets himself literally thrown to the lions. Wisely, the lions decide they don't want to eat a man of God and as a result they get to eat the people who accused Daniel instead. In fact, the Bible says God protected Daniel because he put his faith in Him (verse 23). That's enough of a thought for the day in itself! However, it's also another reminder to us that some issues are worth losing things over. Daniel was prepared to lose his life rather than not worship God. What about us?

I remember that once when I was working in the bank I really blotted my copybook with the area sales manager when I refused to be involved with something that used astrological symbols to market a product. I got the feeling that as long as this man was there, my career was shot to pieces. Six months later, he was made redundant and I was promoted. Not quite a life-on-the-line issue, but the principle is the same. Fight the right battles, trust God and He will stand by you.

Prayer: Help me to be a man of no compromise and to hold the line of faith no matter what. In Jesus' name. Amen.

15/ Men of hope

'May the God of hope fill you with all joy and peace as you trust in him, so that you may overflow with hope by the power of the Holy Spirit.' **Romans 15:13**

'Hope' is a great word. It doesn't just have a particular meaning, it conveys a powerful feeling to those around us. God is a God of hope, and with hope comes joy and peace, but the question is: How can I embrace it? How can I live that way today? The answer is an amazing little phrase: 'as you *trust* in Him.' When you trust Him, there's a release of the power of the Holy Spirit in your life and you overflow with hope.

Trust is probably the most fragile thing in this world – and when it's broken, it's really difficult to rebuild. So, what does it take to trust God, to be a man of hope? Well, there are two things about trust. The first is, it's a risk you take. We love to be in control of our lives, particularly us guys, and when you hand control over to someone else, you take a risk. Actually, when you trust God with your life there is no risk at all – but it's still very difficult to hand Him control. The second thing about trust is that you can't be ordered to trust, it's a choice you have to make. You *choose* to trust someone else. You *choose* to trust God. It's a choice you make and a risk you take. But the end result can be that today you will overflow with hope and the Holy Spirit will release in you joy and peace.

Let's be men of hope today in a broken and lost world!

Prayer: God of hope, I pray that today my faith and trust will increase and You will fill me with Your peace and joy. Amen.

16/Don't lose heart!

'Therefore, since through God's mercy we have this ministry, we do not lose heart.' **2 Corinthians 4:1**

It's so easy to lose heart. Disappointment, depression, despair, or just being down – it seems that just about anything beginning with 'd' can make us lose heart! We're called to be passionate people, but that passion for the ministry God has given us can so easily diminish. And yet it's *because* we have this ministry – which has the power to transform lives, to change anyone and everyone, which can even take someone who seems to be nothing and make them something – it's because we have this ministry that we don't quit. That's what Paul is saying here. If anyone had reason to quit, it was him. He suffered disappointment, he had struggles and challenges – but he kept going.

Winston Churchill was invited to speak on the subject of leadership at a gathering at Bristol University. When he stood up, everyone in the auditorium was expecting an hour's lecture but all he said was two words: 'Don't quit!' And then he sat down. You can sum leadership up in those two words. And the same applies to us. We've been given a ministry that is so amazing, a gospel that has the power to forgive, to heal, to bring about transformation. So, however you're feeling today, whoever has said something to you, or done something, that has left you feeling disappointed, maybe, or down, be encouraged! God has given you a ministry, so don't lose heart. Keep going and embrace all that God has in store for you today.

_____

Prayer: I pray that today my heart will not be pulled down by the things that can discourage me but will be full of Your encouragement, because You believe in me and have given me a ministry. Amen.

_____

17/The work of God

'Then they asked him, "What must we do to do the works God requires?" Jesus answered, "The work of God is this: to believe in the one he has sent."' **John 6:28-29**

They'd seen Jesus do the most extraordinary, profound miracle with some bread and fish, and then He walks on water. Then He tells them: 'Do not work for food that spoils, but for food that endures to eternal life.' Which begs the question for all of us: What does it mean to do the work of God? Now, Jesus could have said, 'Give your tithe', He could have said, 'Go to church, or lots of meetings', He could have said, 'Join this particular group or community' and all of those things might be good things – but you can do them all and still not be doing the work of God, because God really wants us to believe. Without faith, it's impossible to please God; but to believe in God, in the One He has sent, is the real deal.

So, will you choose today to do the work of God? You need to *believe*. Believe that His purposes and His plans for you today will be worked out in your life. Believe that the place where you've 'set your foot' is where the kingdom of God will come. Believe that Jesus is for you and not against you. Believe that He will work in you and through you to establish His kingdom. Be a believer today so that you can do the work of God, because the Son of God has given you all authority as you believe in Him.

Prayer: Lord, increase my faith in You today. Help me to believe that, wherever I set my foot today, Your kingdom will come through me and Your work will progress. Amen.

18/Living it large

'The thief comes only to steal and kill and destroy; I have come that they may have life, and have it to the full.' **John 10:10**

Living life to the full, living it large, living it up is what Christianity is all about. And embracing the present moment is key. But there is someone who seeks to steal, kill and destroy that moment and his strategy has always been the same: he'll either use things to make you keep dwelling on your past - lack of forgiveness, guilt, regret or failure - or things that cast a shadow over the future, like fear or anxiety.

Christianity is all about embracing the present moment. *Today* is the day of salvation. You don't have to allow the enemy to steal, kill and destroy God's life in you today. So, embrace the moment and live it large, live it to the full - and if anything relating to the past or the future is stealing God's life from you, just invite His life and His presence

to invade your life today and live it large,
in Jesus' name.

Prayer: I pray that today more of Your life will be in me than stuff that will frustrate and crush Your presence in me. I pray that I will embrace the moment and release more of Your life in me and through me. Amen.

Here is the test to find whether your mission on Earth is finished: if you're alive, it isn't.
RICHARD BACH

19/Cracking on

'Blessed is the one who perseveres under trial because, having stood the test, that person will receive the crown of life that the Lord has promised to those who love him.'
James 1:12

A couple of years ago, I and a few mates decided to do some epic endurance challenges for charity. One of the things we did was cycle from Calais to Nice. I have to say at this point that when I agreed to do it I hadn't realised that the Alps were in the way! All I had in my mind was the south of France and baguettes … Training for the ride was a killer. I had to get a huge number of miles into my legs and get used to being in pain for hours on end. To get to the top of a pass means cycling constantly uphill for several hours at a time. In the event, we did a thousand miles and climbed about 90,000 feet.

I'll never forget the feeling when I finally got to Nice and got off my bike for the last time, though I can't quite describe it. It was a mixture of relief, exhilaration, a sense of achievement and exhaustion, all rolled into one. I kind of wondered if that is what it will be like one day when we finally kneel before Jesus, having finished the race of life. All I do know is that, as a life lesson, training for the ride, putting in the effort and suffering the pain were well worth it at the end. I hope that when this world comes to an end we will all be able to say the same about the decisions we made and the effort we put in as we pursued Jesus and His kingdom.

Prayer: Help me to endure under pressure, to take discomfort in my stride and strive to follow Jesus, until the day He calls me home. Amen.

20/Listen up!

'My dear brothers and sisters, take note of this: everyone should be quick to listen, slow to speak and slow to become angry.' **James 1:19**

When I was at Bible college, there was a bloke there who knew everything. You know the type. As soon as anyone started to discuss anything, he would cut right in with an opinion. During lectures, some esteemed expert on a finer point of theology would be explaining something, only for this guy to storm in with his own take on the subject. Usually, when the lecturer responded, you could tell that this guy wasn't listening. Instead, he was already formulating his reply in his head before the expert had even finished speaking. Suffice it to say, he never finished the course and didn't go on to lead a church – no prizes for guessing why.

The Bible tells us to spend more time listening than speaking. This is tough for most men – we're experts on everything! To tell the truth, though, the more time you spend listening, the more likely you are to have something worthwhile to say. Try it out sometime, especially at home!

Prayer: I will aim to be slow to speak and quick to listen. Give me opportunities this week to really listen to people and help me in my daily life of faith to spend time listening to You, God. Amen.

I like to listen. I have learned a great deal from listening carefully. Most people never listen.
ERNEST HEMINGWAY

21/Being a doer

'Do not merely listen to the word ...
Do what it says.' **James 1:22**

A huge number of Christians make what are actually commands a matter of prayer and the need for supernatural help. Let me explain. The Bible tells us to be kind and forgiving, not to lie, to be slow to anger, faithful and grafted into the Vine. It tells us to be compassionate, to fast, to lay hands on the sick and to be generous. None of these things (and there are many more) are optional. We are simply told to do them and crack on with it.

I didn't know whether to laugh or cry once when I visited a church where the worship and the sermon were on the theme of loving God and your neighbour and, after the service, all these rows broke out in the church car park because some people had blocked other people in!

And then there was the time I was at a Christian conference and nipped into the Pizza Express over the road. The waiter, not knowing I was attending the conference, joked that he could always tell when it was a Christian event. 'Why's that?' I foolishly asked. 'Easy,' he replied. 'They all order water, they don't tip and we get more complaints than usual.' Enough said.

Prayer: Let my words and my actions be in harmony with what I believe. I want to be a doer as well as a listener. Amen.

22/Mixing it up

'My brothers and sisters, believers in our glorious Lord Jesus Christ must not show favouritism. Suppose a man comes into your meeting wearing a gold ring and fine clothes, and a poor man in filthy old clothes also comes in. If you show special attention to the man wearing fine clothes and say, "Here's a good seat for you," but say to the poor man, "You stand there" or "Sit on the floor by my feet," have you not discriminated among yourselves and become judges with evil thoughts?' **James 2:1-4**

We put people in a box within seconds of seeing them. How they're dressed, the car they pulled up in, the watch on their wrist, the colour of their skin, their weight and build, their smell ... All these things tell us what kind of person they are – according to our own measure, of course. When they open their mouths we make another judgment and so it goes on. What tends to happen then is that we decide pretty quickly whether we are going to invest time in that person or not. It happens in the church, the gym - it can be even more acute at work, where someone's position in the company is yet another factor.

James, however, is clear: we should treat all people the same and we are not to judge anyone on appearances. Now, that may be tough if you're the top gun at work, but we don't have a choice in this. It's the same at church on Sunday. Why not make a decision to sit with the person who doesn't quite fit with you, or to grab some time with them in the week? At your workplace, what about having lunch with someone of lower rank than you? The bottom line is this, I think: we were meant to spend more time with people, but especially with people who 'aren't as good as us'.

Prayer: Give me opportunities to spend more time with people, especially those who are different from me. Show me also how I can tackle prejudice and favouritism when I see it. In Jesus' name. Amen.

23/Choices

'But if you harbour bitter envy and selfish ambition in your hearts, do not boast about it or deny the truth. Such "wisdom" does not come down from heaven but is earthly, unspiritual, demonic. For where you have envy and selfish ambition, there you find disorder and every evil practice. But the wisdom that comes from heaven is first of all pure; then peace-loving, considerate, submissive, full of mercy and good fruit, impartial and sincere. Peacemakers who sow in peace reap a harvest of righteousness.' **James 3:14-18**

In a previous devotion we talked about praying for wisdom. We know from the Bible that God answers this prayer and is keen to do so. You then have a choice: you can use the wisdom God gives you for good or for ill. It really is down to you. In this case, 'ill' means for your own advantage. I've seen this loads, both in and outside the church – incredibly skilled and talented blokes basically using God-given gifts of leadership, vision and persuasion to promote themselves at other people's expense. The Bible calls this 'selfish ambition'. The alternative is to use what God has given you to bring life. The marks of this are made really clear: you are characterised by grace and mercy and all the fruit of the Spirit.

Perhaps it would be good throughout today to think about what you pray for and why. Think also about the decisions you make. Are they all for your benefit or for the benefit of others? How would your mates describe you? Would they say you are generous and considerate or selfish and inconsiderate? So much of the Christian life is about how we choose to live and act with what God has given us. It really is down to us.

Prayer: May my reputation from now on be that of a man who is selfless and full of grace. May my decisions be based on what is best for others and not what is best for me. Amen.

24/Planning ahead

'Now listen, you who say, "Today or tomorrow we will go to this or that city, spend a year there, carry on business and make money." Why, you do not even know what will happen tomorrow. What is your life? You are a mist that appears for a little while and then vanishes. Instead, you ought to say, "If it is the Lord's will, we will live and do this or that."' James 4:13-15

Life is short. Fact. Not a cheery start to the day if you're reading this first thing, but you can't dispute the truth of the statement. I've been to enough funerals (and taken enough!) to know that towards the end of their life people are shocked at how quickly it has passed. That is why we ought to be careful about how we are spending our time and the reasoning we are basing our life choices on. James is simply saying here that if your plans are all based on what will get you the best material gains, they're stupid, frankly. After all, you could make a decision that has a major impact on your life only to find out within a month that your time – in this life – has run out.

So, what James says is this: Commit your plans to God and do what He wants you to do, not just what you think is a brilliant idea. Of course, your brilliant idea may be from God – it's just that you should really make sure that it is before you press the 'go' button. In my head I've got the classic scenario from *Only Fools and Horses*. Del Boy buys a load of t-shirts at a knock-down price, thinking he can make a few quid. The t-shirts say: 'Free Nelson Mandela'. You can guess what happens next – and there endeth today's thought.

Prayer: Help me to live according to what pleases You. I commit my decisions to You, God, and I pray that You'll help me to follow Your will for my life and not just pursue my own plans that I haven't checked through with You. Amen.

[WHO'S THE BOSS?]

25/The One in charge

'Therefore God exalted him to the highest place and gave him the name that is above every name, that at the name of Jesus every knee should bow, in heaven and on earth and under the earth, and every tongue acknowledge that Jesus Christ is Lord, to the glory of God the Father.' **Philippians 2:9-11**

When I was working in banking as a salesman, I discovered that one of my new clients was a professional medium. Talking with her and being confronted with such a stark battle between what seemed to be the forces of darkness and light I asked her who she thought was in charge in the spirit world. A month went by and she failed to turn up for her next appointment. I bumped into her in the banking hall a few months later and I asked why she had never shown up. The answer blew my mind. She told me she had asked her guides who was in charge and the answer had come back, 'The Christ is in charge'! More than that, they told her that if she ever spoke to me again, they wouldn't communicate with her any longer. That is both awesome and amazing, and a brilliant reminder to me and all of us that Jesus is truly the One to whom every knee will bow! What is more, He's our brother and friend! That's truly humbling and totally inspiring.

Just as a closing word, I would add that much wisdom is needed when dealing with this kind of issue. In the words of many stunt shows: 'Don't try this at home but talk to your pastor'. And remember: we are *not* to try and contact spirits.

Prayer: Thank You, God, that Jesus has the name above every name and is the One to whom every knee will one day bow. Thank You for the confidence this gives me to really live unashamed for You. Amen.

26/Don't listen

'Once you were alienated from God and were enemies in your minds because of your evil behaviour. But now he has reconciled you by Christ's physical body through death to present you holy in his sight, without blemish and free from accusation.' **Colossians 1:21-22**

Sometimes it's good to remember the most basic truths of our faith. I don't know what's going on in the day-to-day of your life, but I can hazard a pretty good guess about a number of things. Show me a bloke who hasn't struggled with porn and I'm the Queen of Sheba. Show me a married man who hasn't had a row with his wife and been in the wrong and I'll eat my eight-year-old trainers. You get the point. Life throws stuff at us and sin happens.

It's at those moments that the enemy loves to whisper in our ear that God is finished with us. He loves to tell us that God thinks we're rubbish and doesn't hear our prayers. He loves to tell us that we're spiritually useless and good for nothing. As a result, blokes become apathetic and give up the fight. The enemy knows which buttons to press and he does it mercilessly. What he wants you to do is quit. Simple as that.

Remember the truth today. Jesus got nailed to the cross instead of you – and as a result, when God looks at you, as a follower of Jesus, He sees His Son. So, walk free, hold your head up high and crack on! You're a son of the Living God, adopted into the family of heaven, free to get out there and serve Jesus.

Prayer: Thank You, God, for Jesus. Thank You that when You look at me, You see Him. Frankly, that is amazing! Help me to understand it and live in the light of it. Amen.

27/Thankfulness

'So then, just as you received Christ Jesus as Lord, continue to live your lives in him, rooted and built up in him, strengthened in the faith as you were taught, and overflowing with thankfulness.' **Colossians 2:6-7**

Thankfulness. The counter-cultural word of the day. Let's face it, most people are whingers. Sit in any staffroom and people will be moaning about the organisation and their bosses. Watch a soap opera – not for long, or you'll feel like doing yourself in! – and it's mostly based on complaint. The same applies to any queue anywhere, and especially any queue where you have to spend money when you get to the front of it! The call of the kingdom is to live to another set of values. The Bible here tells us to live a life that's overflowing with thankfulness!

Now, we've got to think this through for a minute. How do you overflow with thankfulness when you've just had a massive car repair bill or some bad news about your health from the doctor? Tough one, that. I think it starts by being thankful in the everyday stuff and training your head to respond differently to all that's around you. If you can find things to be thankful for when you wake up – *and* when you find yourself in a traffic jam – you are more likely to be thankful and find a way through when really bad stuff happens. So, let's start, as men, to be thankful for the small things and work our way up!

Prayer: Thank You, Father, for all the good things in my life. *[Pause for a while and think them through.]* Help me to live a life that overflows with thanks. In Jesus' name. Amen.

28/Keep looking up!

'Since, then, you have been raised with Christ, set your hearts on things above, where Christ is, seated at the right hand of God.'
Colossians 3:1

When a matador fights a bull, he stacks the odds in his favour. First of all, the banderilleros come in and wear the bull out as they charge around on horseback. They also thrust short spears into his neck and shoulders. In the end, as a result of blood loss, muscle damage and exhaustion, the bull can only look at the ground. It is then that the matador comes in and, after doing a few flashy moves, basically finishes off an animal that is totally knackered.

Have you noticed that the enemy tries the same trick with you? In this case, the spears are things like disappointment, 'friendly fire', porn, anger, finances etc. The whole time this is going on, it's like he is saying to you, 'Look at the ground! Look at the ground!' He wants to smother our vision of

God. He wants to weaken our relationship with God until he is ready to move in for the kill. The whole time, however, the Holy Spirit is calling us to keep looking up at Jesus. So, listen to His voice, not the voice of the enemy. Keep looking up, keep a sense of heaven on your shoulder and don't let the enemy use bullfighting tactics on you!

Prayer: I fix my eyes on Jesus and determine to keep looking up today, not down at the ground. Amen.

29/Called to account

'Let the message of Christ dwell among you richly as you teach and admonish one another with all wisdom through psalms, hymns, and songs from the Spirit, singing to God with gratitude in your hearts. And whatever you do, whether in word or deed, do it all in the name of the Lord Jesus, giving thanks to God the Father through him.'
Colossians 3:16-17

We understand stuff like worship and prayer in the Christian life, but what about admonishing one another? That's a different kettle of fish, I reckon. OK, we've probably all been at the pointed end of a comment like 'I'm saying this in love, brother ...' when what they really mean is 'I'm saying this to really do your head in', but these verses aren't talking about that kind of friendly fire. What they're talking about is correcting each other so that we don't fall off the narrow path (Matt. 7:13-14). Personally, I reckon that every man who follows Jesus needs to be in some kind of accountability group. I meet a few blokes regularly and it totally keeps me on the straight and narrow. These guys are really honest with me and I'm honest back. We ask each other about our sex lives, how much we're drinking, what our thought lives are like – the whole deal. When one of us is making a poor decision or heading for some trouble, the other guys will pull him back. It's awesome! The thing is, it means that sometimes you're going to get it in the neck – but if it's in the context of a tight group of mates who have got each other's backs, that's totally OK, isn't it?

Prayer: Help me to be secure enough to take it on the chin when I've been out of line, and secure enough, too, to tell my mates when I think they're heading for trouble. Surround me with some blokes I can journey with through thick and thin. Amen.

[ARMOUR]

30/Strong

'Finally, be strong in the Lord and in his mighty power.' **Ephesians 6:10**

We have a little saying in the CVM office: 'Put yourself in the corner, give yourself a good talking to and crack on!' It sounds harsh for a Christian ministry, I know, but the truth is that sometimes, when we are having a hissy fit, we just need to man up and get on with it. I know there's a time and a place for taking some time out to lick your wounds but, if I'm really honest, I've noticed over a decade of working specifically with men that blokes do have a tendency to sulk and a fight-or-flight mentality. I think that means there are times when we simply need to get a grip on ourselves.

Now, it's at the low moments like this that we need to remind ourselves that our strength ultimately comes from the Living God, not our testosterone. Yes, we may need to give ourselves a talking to, but it's a myth that we alone can sort everything out. So, next time the chips are down and everything is crowding in, put yourself in the corner and give yourself a talking to – and talk to the Living God as well! That's where your strength will come from.

Prayer: Next time the going gets a bit tough, please help me to remember that my strength comes from You. Send Your Holy Spirit to help me sort my head out and keep strong. In Your name I pray. Amen.

Don't whine – laugh.
ROY CASTLE

31/Eyes open

> 'Put on the full armour of God, so that you can take your stand against the devil's schemes. For our struggle is not against flesh and blood, but against the rulers, against the authorities, against the powers of this dark world and against the spiritual forces of evil in the heavenly realms.' **Ephesians 6:11-12**

Make no mistake, we are in a fight – it just seems sometimes, looking around the churches, that no one has noticed there's a war on!

Every now and again I stumble across some crazy conspiracy theory on the internet, usually claiming that UFOs are taking over the world or that our rulers are really lizard people (I kid you not!). What we must not forget, however, is that there *is* a conspiracy, led by an arch-conspirator! The Bible tells us that the enemy is a cunning schemer. More than that, we are told to take our stand against him and his work. What we need to understand, in order to do that, is that we aren't in a straight fight – we have an enemy who uses guerrilla warfare tactics. Far too often we fight the issues that are immediately around us and in front of our faces without realising in the problems and struggles where the real threat is coming from. We need to have our eyes opened to the spiritual realm all around us and learn how to engage in effective warfare against the enemy.

Prayer: Open my eyes to the true nature of the spiritual war that is raging around me. Show me how I can take my stand against the devil and his schemes and struggle effectively against the spiritual forces of darkness in heavenly places. Amen.

32/ Nothing missing

'Therefore put on the full armour of God, so that when the day of evil comes, you may be able to stand your ground, and after you have done everything, to stand.'
Ephesians 6:13

Go into a battle with a bit of armour missing and a part of your body will be vulnerable. That's where the old phrase 'a chink in your armour' comes from. In fact, a medieval knight off for a spot of jousting or cavalry duty would be covered from head to toe in steel plate weighing about 50kg, which often meant he had to be winched onto his unfortunate horse! In the same way, we are told to put on the full armour of God in order to be fully prepped for battle.

Unfortunately, however, many times I see believers with one bit of armour missing. Let me explain. We might be awesome at prayer but never share our faith. We might be well versed in the Bible but lacking in grace and peace etc. The

Bible goes on to tell us just what we need to have in order to stand firm, in the expectation that a day of evil will come. So, make sure there are no chinks in your armour and that (there's no better way to put this!) you've got your spiritual trousers on as well as your shirt when you go out to face the day.

Prayer: I put on the full armour of God so that I can take my stand against the forces of darkness. Show me where there are chinks in my armour and keep me vigilant against the work of the enemy. Amen.

33/Truth and righteousness

'Stand firm then, with the belt of truth buckled round your waist, with the breastplate of righteousness in place.' Ephesians 6:14

It's interesting that the very first two bits of armour the Bible lists involve our integrity. Someone once said that the person you really are is the person you are when no one is looking. Ouch! So true, but really challenging. I think that in essence that's where we need to focus when we look at a verse like this. Let's be honest about who we really are and go from there. First up, truth is absolutely vital. Many of us reading this won't be out-and-out liars but we may be prone to exaggeration or what is often termed 'a little white lie'. What a stupid expression! There's no such thing as a white lie. You're either telling the truth or you're not. Or are there ever shades of grey? Let's commit to speaking straight and being bang on with the truth.

The next bit of armour is the breastplate of righteousness. I guess the question here that we need to honestly ask ourselves is: 'Am I really leading a life that pleases God?' I'm not saying that we need to live like Cromwell's Puritans, but I do believe that the Holy Spirit lets us know when we are a bit out of step with what God wants from us. The trick then is to make the necessary adjustments. If the same thing happens to you as is happening to me as I write this, there may well be one or two things the Holy Spirit is already asking you to deal with!

Prayer: I determine to put on the belt of truth and the breastplate of righteousness, so that I can stand firm against any attack. Amen.

34/Readiness

> 'And with your feet fitted with the readiness that comes from the gospel of peace.' **Ephesians 6:15**

I once went to visit a group of people – all believers – working in a massive open-plan office – and I do mean massive. They all worked in booths made up of dividing screens about five feet tall. One guy, I found out, had worked in the same booth for about seven years. 'Who works in the booth next to you?' I asked him. 'Not a clue', he replied. 'I deal with the people on the next floor.' I was amazed. I'm not being critical here, it was just an eye-opener! This guy (and I found out this was happening all over the workplace) had no reason to talk to the person next to him, so he didn't. Typical bloke in many ways.

The issue, though, is that, while we shouldn't steal from work time, we should be ready to engage with the people around us. You are an ambassador for the King of kings, and perhaps the only person in your immediate orbit who is.

The same applies to our neighbourhood. So, with feet fitted with the readiness that comes from the gospel of peace, let's step out!

Prayer: Give me an opportunity today to share my faith or offer prayer – and give me the words to speak when You do. Amen.

I never worry about action, but only inaction.
WINSTON CHURCHILL

35/Shield

'In addition to all this, take up the shield of faith, with which you can extinguish all the flaming arrows of the evil one.' **Ephesians 6:16**

Faith is the ability to trust God as you step out when you can't see where you're heading or even the next step you will have to take. But what about the flaming arrows – what are they? They can be many different things, of course, but I think in this context we are talking about those things that are the enemy of faith. Perhaps we could name some of them: disappointment, cynicism, doubt, opposition, obstacles and distractions. It seems to me that whenever the enemy wants to dent my faith, there is a constant muttering in the background that goes something like this: 'Did God really say that? Is He really there for you? What if you've got it all wrong?' And so it goes on. It can be tough to keep pressing forward in the face of such a whispering campaign, but that's why we need a robust shield of faith!

What we need to do is make sure that we have the biggest and strongest shield possible, and that's going to mean we need some good muscles to hold it up. So, spend time building those faith muscles! Do things that, step by step, stretch your faith. When I trained for the marathon, I could only run a mile at first. All I did was run 10% further every week until I could do the whole 26 miles. Building our faith is the same, so let's start building it, starting today. What can you 'be in faith' for, trust God for?

Prayer: Holy Spirit, prompt me with something I can 'be in faith' for and inspire me to keep stepping up and out in faith in the weeks ahead. Amen.

36/Sword strike

'Take the helmet of salvation and
the sword of the Spirit, which is the
word of God.' **Ephesians 6:17**

Next up in the armoury is your headgear and
the only offensive weapon of the lot: your sword.
Being an ex-biker (and sometime Alpine cyclist),
I can vouch for the need for a good bit of head
protection. In this case, it is standing firm in
knowing that you are part of God's family, you are
one of the redeemed and your destiny is secure.
If you know that, I reckon you can face anything.
A good discipline to have is to regularly remind
yourself of the day you met Jesus and remind
yourself of the fundamentals of your faith. It's so
easy to lose ground in the basic areas as life and
faith become increasingly complex. I love the
response of Karl Barth, the great theologian who
wrote the epic *Church Dogmatics*, when he was
asked what all his great learning had taught him.
His reply was classic: 'Jesus loves me. This I know,
for the Bible tells me so.'

And that brings me to the sword. Nice one, guys, for reading this with me and being part of a brotherhood all over the world who have committed to read at least one verse a day from the Bible and focus on it. It's getting the Word of God into our DNA that will help us fight. When Jesus was tempted in the desert, He hit back with the Word of God. Not a bad way to go ... So, let's get some sword strikes in and start fighting forwards!

Prayer: Remind me, Father, of the day I met You, and keep the memory fresh in my mind. Thank You that I am part of the family of heaven and part of a worldwide brotherhood of men who know You. I commit to stay focused on Your Word. Show me how I can use Your words as a weapon against the work of the enemy, and bring them back to my mind when I face temptation and pressure. Amen.

37/Pray up!

'And pray in the Spirit on all occasions with all kinds of prayers and requests. With this in mind, be alert and always keep on praying for all the Lord's people.' **Ephesians 6:18**

I'm an activist through and through. That has its good points and its bad points when it comes to being a disciple of Jesus. I want to get out there and crack on and make stuff happen without pausing for thought. This means that my prayer life can get neglected. It's probably selfish of me in some ways, because in truth I should be praying for my mates and my family, my colleagues at work and people I know who don't yet know Jesus. That's all part of staying spiritually fit and focused on Jesus. To that end, I've started using lists – speaking as someone who never writes lists for anything. Keep one on your phone of people and things to pray through and when you get a moment, read it through. Perhaps have some things you pray for daily and some you pray for weekly etc. Use the Bible as well, and maybe some old hymns. The Bible is brilliant for prayer, particularly the Psalms. So, let's get into a prayer battle, keeping alert and mindful of situations and people that need our prayers!

Prayer: Today I remember before You those who don't know You. *[Go through your list of names.]* **I also remember those in my family and my church who need my prayers just now.** *[Go through the list again.]* **Amen.**

[NOTHING DOING]

38/Out of nothing

'Now the earth was formless and empty, darkness was over the surface of the deep, and the Spirit of God was hovering over the waters. And God said, "Let there be light", and there was light. God saw that the light was good, and he separated the light from the darkness. God called the light 'day', and the darkness he called 'night'. And there was evening, and there was morning – the first day.'
Genesis 1:2-5

The book of Genesis is full of large expanses of nothingness. The idea of nothingness sits at the bottom of its chapters like an anchor dragging across the ocean floor. First there was nothing, and out of nothing God created everything. Humanity lacked nothing but longed for everything. Adam witnessed Eve's first sin – and did nothing. When God questioned their actions, they claimed it was nothing to do with them.

Later, God saw that, apart from Noah, nothing good remained on the earth, and so He destroyed everything. Nothingness, emptiness and darkness cling to the creation story. And yet, as I study Genesis, I see that something in God's character longs to create His finest work out of nothingness. God continually intercepts dark situations with His presence.

There may be situations in your life where you just see darkness. People you're trying to help are addicted to sin, or projects you've launched just seem to be heading nowhere. Be encouraged. God rubs His hands at the prospect of nothingness. To judge from Genesis, nothingness is a place where God is just waiting to run wild!

Prayer: Father, give me hope in the situations where all I see is nothingness. Thank You for Your son, the Lord Jesus, the greatest hope of all. In His name I pray. Amen.

39/Walk this way

'He has showed you, O mortal, what is good. And what does the LORD require of you? To act justly and to love mercy and to walk humbly with your God.' **Micah 6:8**

Some of them were heroes, others were righteous and a few were wise – but only two men 'walked with God'. As we scour the early parts of the Bible and meet the big characters, we see that God allowed men to contribute their own brushstrokes to His already perfect canvas. Much of their early work started as beautiful patterns, with the likes of Adam, Abel and Abraham striving to honour their Maker. But for every step of holiness taken by one biblical character, a marathon of sinfulness is run in the same story. Looking at the mess we often make of our own lives, one has to wonder why God created us in the first place.

But then in the early pages of the Bible we find Noah and Enoch. Something about their lifestyles won God's favour, but what is fascinating is that both of them receive a wonderful accolade even before they complete the tasks for which they are remembered. Noah 'walked with God' before he built the Ark. Enoch 'walked with God' before, uniquely, he was 'taken' from this life.

So, where does this leave you and me, brother? I guess our 'walk with God' looks like a blank canvas today. And we know that if we choose to allow Jesus to take charge of the painting, we also need to pick up a brush ourselves. As this day stretches out before us with its unique blots and blemishes, how can we keep our eyes fixed on the perfect Painter? How can we walk with God?

Prayer: Father, show us how we can walk with You today. In Jesus' name. Amen.

40/Write-off

'But the LORD said to Samuel, "Do not consider his appearance or his height, for I have rejected him. The LORD does not look at the things people look at. People look at the outward appearance, but the LORD looks at the heart."' **1 Samuel 16:7**

A few weeks ago I sat in a city-centre café, waiting for my friend Dan to join me, and watched two women approach the manager to enquire about a part-time job. The first woman came in alone, armed with a smile and a CV. After a brief conversation, she expressed her interest in the position and handed over her life's logbook. The second woman was with her boyfriend. She had exactly the same conversation with the manager and then put her CV in his hands. After the women had left, the bar staff marvelled at how two people could apply for the same job within seconds of each other. I sipped my Diet Coke with one ear on the conversation.

The manager read both CVs and nonchalantly corrected the mistakes, and bantered with his bar staff about how much power he had. Then, without further thought, he tore up one of the CVs and said: 'Well, it's simple. I'm going to interview the girl who came in alone, because the other girl's boyfriend looked pretty rough. I don't want that in here.'

That story may be extreme but the truth is that we write people off so quickly these days. I'm glad the Creator of all things doesn't base His decisions on first impressions like the manager of that café. As you read what the Bible says about the issue, think about how you can bless those around you today.

Prayer: Father, minister to my soul today so that I may show respect to those around me regardless of what they look like. Amen.

41/Lion down

'The Son is the image of the invisible God, the firstborn over all creation. For in him all things were created: things in heaven and on earth, visible and invisible, whether thrones or powers or rulers or authorities; all things have been created through him and for him. He is before all things, and in him all things hold together.'
Colossians 1:15-17

I recently had the pleasure of visiting South Africa. I was moved to tears by many of the things I saw, from the Apartheid Museum and the record of some of the horrific events that plagued the last century to the faithfulness and generosity of the local people. One of the most memorable experiences I had, however, was when I was watching some lions hanging around in a park. (You just don't see that sort of thing back in Wales!) I was standing behind a fence just 10 metres from one male who was lying on the ground tearing at a lump of meat that had once been part of another animal. His mane was dripping with blood but, to be honest, the thought struck me that I could take him in a fight. However, this feeling of superiority quickly evaporated when the lion stood up. He looked much bigger standing up! In fact, he was so unfazed by my presence that he didn't look at me once. The fact is that nothing scares a lion, so he never has to look at anything he doesn't want to.

As I took a few steps back from the fence of humility, another thought struck me. I used to see God as a Being with an exaggerated reputation. However, the fact is that our God has stood up. And as I look at what Jesus did for me on the cross, and what He won for me at the resurrection, I take a few steps back and I see that God is a lot bigger than I thought He was.

Prayer: Father, help me to get a true sense of Your power today. In Jesus' name. Amen.

[BRUISERS]

42/Short accounts!

'Again the Israelites did evil in the eyes of the LORD, and because they did this evil the LORD gave Eglon king of Moab power over Israel. Getting the Ammonites and Amalekites to join him, Eglon came and attacked Israel, and they took possession of the City of Palms. The Israelites were subject to Eglon king of Moab for eighteen years.'
Judges 3:12-14

The period of the Judges is one of turmoil punctuated by spells of peace. In a nutshell, when the people of Israel were on the money, God blessed them and things went well for them. When they took their eyes off the ball, things went badly. In fact, at times they went very badly. In this particular period, they went badly for 18 years and once again (this happened more than a few times) their land was occupied and they were ruled by an oppressor. What would often happen then was that, because things were so grim, the people would cry out to God, who in turn (being very patient and gracious) would raise someone up – a 'judge' – to sort it all out.

The lesson here is that we would do far better to avoid the downturn by staying focused on God all the time. I know this is easier to say than to do, but nevertheless it's far better to keep what we call 'short accounts' with God and live a life that pleases Him. Remember as well that when we rebel, whether in secret or openly, it tends to have a major impact not just on us but on the people around us. For a classic example of this, read the story of Achan sometime in Joshua 7. In that case, one man's sin taints a whole nation! So, keep your head and keep your focus on God.

Prayer: Father, when I make decisions that grieve You, please pull me back or put people alongside me who will help me to stay on the narrow path. Amen.

43/Bruisers for Jesus

'Again the Israelites cried out to the LORD, and he gave them a deliverer – Ehud, a left-handed man, the son of Gera the Benjaminite. The Israelites sent him with tribute to Eglon king of Moab.' **Judges 3:15**

Yesterday, I explained that whenever the people cried out to God for help, He would raise up a 'judge' to sort it all out. Sometimes these people would be like judges in the conventional sense, dispensing justice and wisdom. At other times, as circumstances required, God would raise up a bruiser like Samson, or in this case Ehud, the left-handed assassin. Ehud, it seems to me, was probably an unexpected choice and I like that! I love the fact that God can use people we wouldn't have thought of as leaders who do amazing exploits for Him. I like the detail here of him being left-handed, and also that when we first meet him he is just a messenger and probably seems expendable! God, of course, had other plans ...

My message today is this: Be ready to go into action for God. You may not be the obvious choice, you may be a man-in-waiting and have been so for many years. Be assured, though, that God has seen you and when He needs you to spring into action, He will let you know. So, don't be discouraged, stay faithful, keep your head and be prepared!

Prayer: Thank You, Father, that You use the faithful and the unexpected. I commit to stay faithful to You and ready for You to use me whenever You call upon me to serve You. Amen.

44/Red mist

'But on reaching the stone images near Gilgal he himself went back to Eglon and said, "Your Majesty, I have a secret message for you."'
Judges 3:19

As we continue with Ehud, we jump to the point where he has delivered the tribute to Eglon and is making his way back home. Something happens at Gilgal, however. Read the rest of the story through when you get a minute. In a nutshell, Ehud goes back and stabs Eglon with a sword. In fact, the Bible says that Eglon was so fat and Ehud so full-on that the blade sank into his stomach so far that his guts closed over the hilt! So, what happened? The clue is what Ehud saw at Gilgal. This was the place where Joshua had led the people into the promised land and had ordered them to set up 12 memorial stones, one for each tribe of Israel, as a reminder of God's faithfulness. It was also where the men had been circumcised and had made their commitment to walk with God. Now, however, there were idols there.

From what happened next, I'm pretty convinced that Ehud saw red. He was so mad at what was happening that he went back and took Eglon out!

So, what about us? What are we getting righteously angry about – or are we sleepwalking into apathy and inaction? Personally, I think that believing men need to get a bit worked up about things and make our presence felt. Ehud, a lowly messenger, did – and as a result the people went free for 80 years!

Prayer: Father, show me Your heart for injustice and show me what You would like me to get stirred up about. Then give me the courage to be a doer and make a difference. Amen.

45/Wrong turning

'One evening David got up from his bed and walked around on the roof of the palace. From the roof he saw a woman bathing. The woman was very beautiful, and David sent someone to find out about her. The man said, "She is Bathsheba, the daughter of Eliam and the wife of Uriah the Hittite." Then David sent messengers to get her. She came to him, and he slept with her. (Now she was purifying herself from her monthly uncleanness.) Then she went back home.' **2 Samuel 11:2-4**

I've often mused on this story. I've wondered how many times David took a cheeky walk on the roof of the palace when there was a bit of bathing going on. I've wondered how many times he played games in his mind and slowly but surely numbed and blunted his ability to hold the line. I've wondered, too, how intoxicated he was by his power, by his ability to get a girl and sleep with her whenever he wanted. I know this: I'm no king but I need to be careful I don't take a wrong turning that leads to a massive collision in my life. I've got a few mates who have thrown everything away in a moment of lust. I've wondered about them as well. I've wondered how many times they flirted with the idea of crossing the line until the inevitable happened. One thing's for sure: you don't wake up one day and decide to commit adultery. If you go through that door, you will have opened it many months or years earlier.

So, take today as a reminder to hold the line. If you know you are starting to take a wrong turning, talk to a mate and get it prayed through. Better to be honest now than be well and truly done over in a few months' time ...

Prayer: Show me, Father, if I have taken a wrong turning and give me the strength I need to pull myself back from the brink. Help me, too, to be there for other guys who I can see are struggling with this just now. In Jesus' name. Amen.

46/Murderous sin

'In the morning David wrote a letter to Joab and sent it with Uriah. In it he wrote, "Put Uriah out in front where the fighting is fiercest. Then withdraw from him so he will be struck down and die."' **2 Samuel 11:14-15**

So, David has sex with Bathsheba and she falls pregnant. The next problem to face is that she is already married. So, what does David do? He makes sure that her husband, a loyal warrior, a man devoted to duty, is put in the front line and left to die. Nice touch!

So, what's this all about? It's about a good man who has numbed his conscience. It's about a good man whose decision to take a wrong turning is leading him to hell. It's about the way your sin takes you to places you don't want to go. And that's the bottom line. Remember this thought and get it under your skin: sin will take you down a road you will one day wish you had never even looked down, let alone journeyed down. For David, it led in effect to murder. For most of us, it leads to lies and to a numbed conscience that allows us to commit even greater acts of sin the next time.

It's simple, really – just don't take that path in the first place!

Prayer: May my walk be straight and my heart kept pure. Please protect me from wrong turnings and toxic decisions. Amen.

47/Consequences

"Then David said to Nathan, "I have sinned against the LORD." Nathan replied, "The LORD has taken away your sin. You are not going to die. But because by doing this you have shown utter contempt for the LORD, the son born to you will die.""

2 Samuel 12:13-14

David has sinned, Bathsheba is pregnant and Uriah the loyal soldier is dead. God sends a prophet to rebuke David and deliver some devastating news: the price for his sin is the death of his newborn son. After a short illness lasting seven days, the baby dies, exactly as the prophet had said he would.

Of course, we live post-cross and resurrection. In Jesus we have a man who took the hit for all of the wrong turnings we take, no matter what. Nonetheless, this story reminds us that our wrong turnings also have consequences for us. Let's man up about it: have an affair or give in to a moment of what is basically lust and you will devastate your family. They may never totally get over it. Bend the rules at work and it could cost you your reputation or even your job. Use porn and you may get addicted – I could go on. So, the best strategy is to get some good blokes around you and keep each other going as well as sticking close to God. I keep saying this, but that's because it's the only way forward. Your sin has consequences. Thank God you know Christ so you can find a way through any mess that you cause!

Prayer: I know, God, that my actions have consequences in this life, so please help me to stay on the narrow path. Thank You that even though my actions do have an impact, through the cross I can know forgiveness and find a way through. Amen.

48/Get over it

'Make every effort to live in peace with everyone and to be holy; without holiness no one will see the Lord. See to it that no one falls short of the grace of God and that no bitter root grows up to cause trouble and defile many.'

Hebrews 12:14-15

I remember watching one of those Mafia movies where the godfather says something like 'Revenge is a dish best served cold'. In other words, when you're wronged by someone you don't just rush to get your own back, you wait however long it takes – until you can exact the sweetest, completest revenge. A lot of blokes are like that. I know guys who have never forgiven a member of their family – even a brother – and for years have looked for a way to get back at them. I've seen this attitude in the workplace as well. In the bank once, one guy said to me, after one of the bosses had told him off, that he was going to treat him like he was his best mate 'and then do his legs when the time is right'. Nasty stuff.

That's not the way we roll as followers of Jesus. Our standard operating procedure is to forgive, forget and go the extra mile to make friendships even with those who have wronged us. If someone has hurt us, we forgive, in case bitterness gets a grip on us. Why? Simple. Because we are told to and because our example is Jesus, who while being nailed to a lump of wood, with every right to retaliate, instead forgave. So, next time you feel the angst rising up, get over yourself and it!

Prayer: Help me to be a peacemaker and not a warmonger. Help me to show grace and mercy to all people. Amen.

49/Take a hit

'Blessed are the peacemakers, for
they will be called children of God.'
Matthew 5:9

So, what *is* a peacemaker? I think of people
like Terry Waite, who in the pursuit of peace
in the Middle East was held hostage in Beirut
for nearly five years, much of it in isolation.
Very few of us guys will ever be called on to go
through what he did, but we still have a role to
play in bringing peace and it's usually the tough
option and it can be painful. A peacemaker is
someone who is prepared to suffer themselves
in order to bring peace.

What about family rows? What do you do at the
moment? Are you the one who steps in and sorts
it out or do you sulk or make things worse? What
about work disputes? Are you the guy who brings
the sides together or are you the one who looks
for the angle and what advantage he can get
out of it? It seems to me that our role model in
peacemaking is ultimately Jesus, who of course

could be confrontational when necessary but who was also prepared to pay even the ultimate price in his pursuit of peace. I think making peace has a really high value to God, which is why men who do it are known as His sons.

Prayer: Show me the times when I need to step up and take a hit to bring peace. Holy Spirit, prompt me when You need me to take action to bring peace into tough situations. Amen.

50/Don't be soft

'Peace I leave with you; my peace I give you. I do not give to you as the world gives. Do not let your hearts be troubled and do not be afraid.'
John 14:27

Getting stressed or anxious about stuff is a particularly nasty thing for men. This isn't because we suffer more than women but because we tend to suffer in silence and wear a mask. God, however, who knows what we are like and looks straight into our hearts has provided for us some hugely encouraging words. At the time Jesus spoke them, He was mainly directing them to a church and band of brothers that was soon to find itself facing stiff persecution whilst being apparently without its founding leader.

Just before this verse, though, Jesus talks about the coming of the Holy Spirit and then straight after this verse, He tells them that one day He will be coming back. In other words, Jesus is emphasising to us that in the face of the worst kind of stress, there is a place of inner peace and that we aren't as alone as we might think we are.

So what does it mean for us guys who may not be facing the sharp end of persecution but still may face antagonism for our faith in the workplace or go through periods when everything is crowding in on us? It means, quite simply, that in those moments, we can call on the Holy Spirit to give us peace. It means that we can remember that God, who cannot lie, is still there. It means that even when the chips are down and the wheels are coming off, there is a way through.

Prayer: Please give me the peace of Jesus. Help me to respond to confrontation and adversity in a robust but peace-filled way. Help me to model something different and counter-cultural in the way I handle pressure. Please remind me, in the toughest times, that I am never alone. Amen.

[ALIENS]

51/Hated?

'If the world hates you, keep in mind that it hated me first. If you belonged to the world, it would love you as its own. As it is, you do not belong to the world, but I have chosen you out of the world. That is why the world hates you.' **John 15:18-19**

Tough one, this, to ponder on. The Bible says that the world hates us as followers of Jesus because the world first hated Him and He has 'chosen us out of the world ...' It's telling us that we are so different from the world and what it offers that we don't belong. We're like displaced persons. More than that, not everyone is going to get us and what we stand for and people certainly won't always react to us in the most positive way! There's not much to say about this except 'Get used to it!' It's absolutely true that as followers of Jesus we live by a different code of honour and a different set of values. The things the world finds important – material goods, status etc – are the very things God finds totally insignificant (unless

He determines to use them for a greater good
– eg He might give you wealth so that you can
use it for the kingdom, or status so that you can
bring a kingdom influence to bear) but, after all,
often historically it has been the poorest – even
the most despised (at the time) – who have been
most influential for God.

The mere fact of this will at times annoy people
and frustrate them. The fact that you don't swear
or cheat may alienate them. The fact that you
don't want to do the lottery or go into certain
shops may put you at odds with them. It's just a
given, the way we are called to live – opposition is
part of the journey. The trick is to keep your head
and understand where the opposition comes
from and why it happens. After all, our struggle is
not against flesh and blood …

**Prayer: I understand that in this
life there will be opposition
because I follow Jesus. Despite
this, I will not yield and I
will follow You with all my
heart and strength. Amen.**

52/Passing through

'Dear friends, I urge you, as foreigners and exiles, to abstain from sinful desires, which wage war against your soul.' **1 Peter 2:11**

Shortly after becoming a follower of Jesus, I had this really strange experience one day of feeling very homesick. It was strange because I was at home at the time and surrounded by my family! I found myself sitting in my chair feeling totally displaced and out of sorts and not quite sure why I felt so melancholy. After all, I'm not really a melancholy kind of bloke – normally my cup is half full rather than half empty – so this was a bit weird. It was while I was praying that I finally got it. Deep in my heart, I heard what I now recognise as the still, small (but firm and clear) voice of the Holy Spirit speaking to me: 'You're not home yet, son. That's why you feel this way.' And that's the truth! As soon as you give your life to Jesus, as soon as you commit to God for eternity, you no longer belong to this world. The truth is that you are passing through and that real life is yet to come. So, whatever you are doing now, whatever you are getting on with, do it with a sense of heaven on your shoulder because that is now where you ultimately belong.

Prayer: Thank You, Father, that I belong to You and that my destiny is to be with You for eternity. Help me to keep this life, with all its ups and downs and all its trappings, in perspective and to maintain a sense of heaven as my home, my destination. Amen.

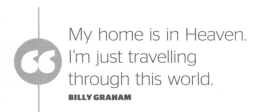

My home is in Heaven. I'm just travelling through this world.
BILLY GRAHAM

53/Citizens of heaven

'For, as I have often told you before and now tell you again even with tears, many live as enemies of the cross of Christ. Their destiny is destruction, their god is their stomach, and their glory is in their shame. Their mind is set on earthly things. But our citizenship is in heaven. And we eagerly await a Saviour from there, the Lord Jesus Christ.' **Philippians 3:18-20**

Philippi was a Roman colony. Let me explain. It was a place where Roman soldiers who had served their time settled in retirement. They were given land and a pension and, after a lifetime of fighting for the empire, could live out their old age in relative peace. So, this is explosive stuff. In a place where people gloried in Roman culture and behaved as if they actually were in Rome, Paul is effectively saying: 'Stuff Rome, you belong to heaven. Have nothing to do with all the stuff you see going on in your city!' There were probably former Roman soldiers among the converts in Philippi, and to that extent this is a radical and even life-threatening call to live differently. That's how the early Christians saw it and called it. If you know Jesus, you live differently, no matter what pressure is put on you to conform.

If an ex-member of the Praetorian Guard can do it (and at least 500 of them lived in Philippi, so one of them at least may well have known Jesus), then so can most of us in 21st-century Britain – a great deal harder in some cultures, I know.

Prayer: Help me to live a truly counter-cultural life, to live as a citizen of heaven in my heart. Amen.

[GENEROSITY]

54/ Charity begins at home?

'Now about the collection for the Lord's people: do what I told the Galatian churches to do. On the first day of every week, each one of you should set aside a sum of money in keeping with your income, saving it up, so that when I come no collections will have to be made.'
1 Corinthians 16:1-2

If you have a family of your own, you have a massive responsibility towards it – and yet, just maybe, the expression 'Charity begins at home' is one of the more dangerous things we can say. Why? Because it gives us an excuse to be tight. In these verses we are told to set aside a sum of money each week to give away. It's as simple as that – it's not an option but a command. My own view is that we should think of a sum we would be comfortable giving and then give a bit more. In terms of a percentage, well, 10% is the biblical benchmark and many of us could probably give a bit more than that. Being generous with our money affects so many other things. It affects how people view us, it affects how we see the world and even the way we look at and speak of others. In my experience, the happiest people I have met have also been the most generous. There's a definite link.

So, practise generosity and look at the level of your giving – it's commanded of us and it's a spiritually healthy thing to do, and it's the only proper response to the generosity God has shown us.

Prayer: Thank You, God, that You have been so generous to me. Thank You for all the things You have blessed my life with. Please keep my heart generous and help me to hold my money and my material possessions lightly. Amen.

55/Share the wealth!

'Share with the Lord's people who are in need. Practise hospitality.'
Romans 12:13

There's this family I know who haven't celebrated Christmas on Christmas Day as a family for years. In fact, most years they celebrate it with a bunch of people they don't know – and spend most of the time peeling potatoes or washing up. That's because they spend the day feeding the blokes at the local homeless shelter for men. I met another guy recently who, in the process of selling his car, found out about a bloke who badly needed one. So, rather than sell it, he gave it away. I like that and I find it challenging. When God has touched your life with His grace, what else can you do but be generous with your time and your possessions?

It's all linked to some of the themes we've been looking at. If this world is not our true home and the stuff we have is truly temporary, why do we hang on to it all so much? I know this is really challenging stuff and we won't all agree with what I'm saying, but at the very least let your heart be open to the idea of being more generous and giving. At the very, very least, why not look out for those in your church who are in greater need than you and find a way to bless them with your time, help and/or money? What about hospitality? How about having some people over who could really use a good meal and some company? Or how about making your home available for a youth group or church meeting of some kind?

I know we need to be wise, but don't let that be an excuse for doing nothing!

Prayer: Show me where I can do more and challenge my heart, where it is selfish, to be more open and generous to those in need around me. Amen.

[DEFENDERS AND HELPERS]

56/Listen, son

'Learn to do right; seek justice. Defend the oppressed. Take up the cause of the fatherless; plead the case of the widow.' **Isaiah 1:17**

In the UK alone, there are about 4,000 children waiting to be adopted at any given time, and in a typical year over 47,000 are placed in foster care. In Haiti, it's estimated, there are over a million children who have lost one or both parents! These are pretty tough statistics. It's hard to get your head around this and to know what to do. What I do know is that God has called us to do something about it and what I do know is that men have a real role to play in fathering and mentoring.

Perhaps God is calling you to adopt or foster. If so, that's great! Perhaps, however, you aren't in a position to take such a step. In that case, what can or should you do? At the very least, as a first step, you could pray about it. Then, perhaps, you could get involved in sponsoring a child in a developing country and/or investing some time in youth work or in mentoring some younger guys who have no male role models and could do with your time. We've focused here on the 'fatherless' element in the verse. Go on, ask this question of yourself: What can and should I do to make a difference as a commitment to following Jesus?

Our faith is about doing the stuff and taking action, so let's, as men, lead the way!

Prayer: Help me to be a father to the fatherless, at the very least as a role model. Help me to be a mentor to guys who really need that kind of input. Amen.

57/Set 'em free!

'The Spirit of the Lord is on me, because he has anointed me to proclaim good news to the poor. He has sent me to proclaim freedom for the prisoners and recovery of sight for the blind, to set the oppressed free, to proclaim the year of the Lord's favour.' **Luke 4:18-19**

The law of jubilee was one of the most profound laws that God ever put in place for the people of Israel. Every 49 years, a horn was to be blown: people who were working as slaves to pay off their debts were to be set free and land that had been sold to pay debts was to be returned to its original owners. It's a complex law (you can read about it in Leviticus 25 and 27), but the bottom line was that it was meant to be the foundation of a just and fair society. The evidence is that it was a law the people of the time conveniently forgot – probably because it was so tough. When Jesus started His ministry by proclaiming 'the year of the Lord's favour', it was basically a call to live by the principle of jubilee – to set captives free, to pray for miracles, to help the poor. He was calling His followers to be the most radical, life-giving people.

I think us men have such a key role to play in this. If all of us were truly to live as Jesus called us to, the world would be a different place!

Prayer: Show me how I can be a man of jubilee and live according to Your Word in the place where You have called me to be. Amen.

[SHEEP-FINDER]

58/Lost and found

'Then Jesus told them this parable:
"Suppose one of you has a hundred
sheep and loses one of them.
Doesn't he leave the ninety-nine in
the open country and go after the
lost sheep until he finds it?"'
Luke 15:3-4

I have to admit it, I'm a reluctant evangelist. I
find it tough to tell people about Jesus. I find it
hard to make small-talk and there's nothing I find
more difficult than cold-calling. I'm just not wired
that way. I do very little of the door-knocking
stuff, if any – and yet I do share my faith. In fact,
I've devoted my life to it. I do it for a number of
reasons: 1) God loves me, 2) He loves everyone
else and 3) the consequences if I don't are too
much to bear.

In these verses, Jesus uses a culturally spot-on
example. It came home to me when I thought that
one of my kids had gone missing – they were only
a few months old at the time. It turned out they

were being cuddled by someone in the church hall next door, but for a few moments my heart was in my mouth and I felt sick. I think this must be how God feels for every one of His children who don't know Him. He's so desperate for people to know Him that He sent His Son to die. For that reason, I get out there and I do my bit. So, let's go find some lost sheep and bring them home!

**Prayer: I really want to be able
to share my faith with my mates
and members of my family,
so please show me how best
to go about this and give me
opportunities to tell people
about Jesus, even today! Amen.**

59/Party time

> 'And when he finds it, he joyfully puts it on his shoulders and goes home. Then he calls his friends and neighbours together and says, "Rejoice with me; I have found my lost sheep."' **Luke 15:5-6**

I love these verses. I have in my head an image of a gnarled and dogged shepherd who has trudged for miles over all kinds of tough and hilly terrain to find his lost sheep. I picture him with it slung over his shoulders and a look of relief on his face. For me, that then becomes a picture of the same gnarled-looking guy with his arm round a bloke, homeward bound, looking totally relieved. The bloke who was running in the wrong direction with his life has turned back.

Nothing beats that moment when one of your mates decides to become a brother and follow Jesus. We need to celebrate every single person who gets saved and go the extra mile in order to see them come through. We've got battles to fight, so let's get to it! Perhaps you could gather some blokes in your church and start to do stuff in order to reach out. Perhaps start to pray for your mates who don't know Jesus yet and ask God for an opportunity to share your faith. Let's crack on and make Jesus known!

Pray: Thank You, God, that You massively celebrate every single person who decides to follow Jesus. Make me a man who does his bit to see more celebrations happen! Amen.

60/Standing orders

'Then Jesus came to them and said, "All authority in heaven and on earth has been given to me. Therefore go and make disciples of all nations, baptising them in the name of the Father and of the Son and of the Holy Spirit, and teaching them to obey everything I have commanded you. And surely I am with you always, to the very end of the age."' **Matthew 28:18-20**

Every army at war has standing orders, and we are no exception. In truth, there are two things we have to do for God: worship Him and make Him known. That's it. Simple. As we come to the close of this book, let's get back to our primary role and make the main thing the main thing! There are 62 million people in the UK and only a very small percentage of them know Jesus. So, let's take His final words seriously and get out there! Whether you're a banker, a bin man, a dentist, a van driver, a pilot, a teacher or out of work, God has placed you there as His ambassador to do His work and spread the news that the kingdom of heaven is near. We all have our bit to do.

Note that Jesus here talks about making disciples and not just winning converts. This means that us men need to get alongside other men and pass on what we have learned. It means we need to spend time with people – and go the extra mile in creating that time. My prayer is that all over the UK we will start to hear stories of men, women and kids who have come to faith through a bunch of blokes who never compromised and kept their faith in full focus.

It's a privilege to be part of this movement of men – let's make sure it grows!

Prayer: Help me to worship You, Lord, and make You known. Help me to stay obedient to Your call and do all You have commanded me to do. I take Your standing order to 'go' seriously. Please use me for Your glory and to spread the fame of Jesus. Amen.

BOOK 1

THE MANUAL

POWER/PLEASURE/
POKER/PORK-PIES

More Bible notes for men written by Carl Beech.

Contains:

- 60 daily readings and prayers

- Two guest contributors:
  Andy Frost and MAF pilot
  Bryan Pill

- Themes to encourage and
  challenge you

'Powerful, personal and relevant'
BEAR GRYLLS

ISBN: 978-1-85345-769-2

Also available in ebook formats

Courses and seminars

Publishing and new media

Conference facilities

Transforming lives

CWR's vision is to enable people to experience personal transformation through applying God's Word to their lives and relationships.

Our Bible-based training and resources help people around the world to:
• Grow in their walk with God
• Understand and apply Scripture to their lives
• Resource themselves and their church
• Develop pastoral care and counselling skills
• Train for leadership
• Strengthen relationships, marriage and family life and much more.

Our insightful writers provide daily Bible-reading notes and other resources for all ages, and our experienced course designers and presenters have gained an international reputation for excellence and effectiveness.

CWR's Training and Conference Centre in Surrey, England, provides excellent facilities in an idyllic setting – ideal for both learning and spiritual refreshment.

CWR Applying God's Word
to everyday life and relationships

CWR, Waverley Abbey House,
Waverley Lane, Farnham,
Surrey GU9 8EP, UK

Telephone: **+44 (0)1252 784700**
Email: **info@cwr.org.uk**
Website: **www.cwr.org.uk**

Registered Charity No 294387
Company Registration No 1990308

it's time for a new kind of man

connecting
men to Jesus
& the church to men

Partner with us
Connect a men's group
Start a men's group
Join a movement

Equipping and resourcing you to
share Jesus with the men around you

networking || events | resources || training

cvm.org.uk

CVM is a movement that offers a range of advice,
resources and men's events across the UK and bey
The Hub, Unit 2, Dunston Rd, Chesterfield S41 8XA Tel: 01246 45
Registered Charity in England & Wales (No.1071663)
A Company Ltd by Guarantee (No. 3623498)